HOW THE NUCLEAR ARMS RACE BROUGHT AN END TO THE COLD WAR

History Book for Kids

Children's War & History Books

Speedy Publishing LLC

40 E. Main St. #1156

Newark, DE 19711

www.speedypublishing.com

Copyright 2017

All Rights reserved. No part of this book may be reproduced or used in any way or form or by any means whether electronic or mechanical, this means that you cannot record or photocopy any material ideas or tips that are provided in this book.

In this book, we're going to talk about how and why the nuclear arms race helped to bring an end to the Cold War. So, let's get right to it!

The Cold War between the Soviet Union, also called the U.S.S.R., and the U.S. took place from 1947 through 1991 when the Soviet Union crumbled. The reason it was called the "Cold War" is because the soldiers from both countries didn't directly battle each other. However, there was a tremendous amount of tension between the two nations, which came out in other types of conflicts.

These two superpowers did "battle" in the following ways:

- Military alliances with other countries
- Spying on each other and espionage to gain military and other secret intelligence
- Propaganda in the press
- Strategic economic aid
- Proxy wars, where they were involved behind the scenes when other countries were fighting
- A buildup of arms on both sides, known as the Arms Race

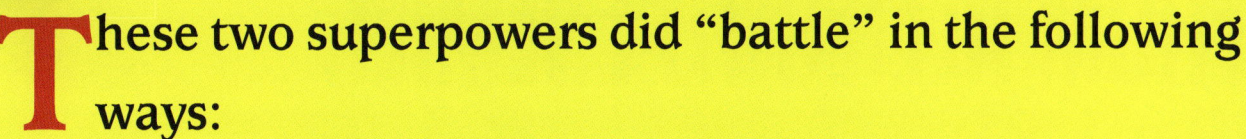

FROM ALLIES TO ENEMIES

During World War II, the U.S.S.R. had been part of the Allied Powers, which included the United States and Britain. The Allied Powers had been fighting against Hitler's Nazi Germany and had won. However, this alliance began to disintegrate as early as the Potsdam Conference.

ALLIED POWERS

During this conference the Allies met to negotiate how Germany would be divided up and occupied. The Potsdam Conference took place between July 17 and August 2nd of 1945 near Berlin, Germany. The "Big Three" were there: Winston Churchill and Clement Attlee, who was Churchill's successor, represented Britain; Harry S. Truman was newly-elected US President and represented the United States; and Joseph Stalin, who was the Soviet Premier represented the Soviet Union.

B ritain and the U.S. were concerned about Joseph Stalin's leadership since he was known for brutality. It was soon clear that the Soviet Union intended to put a barrier between themselves and Western Europe. They began to establish pro-communist governments in the Eastern European countries such as Poland, Bulgaria, and Albania. Eventually, they created a pro-communist government in East Germany as well.

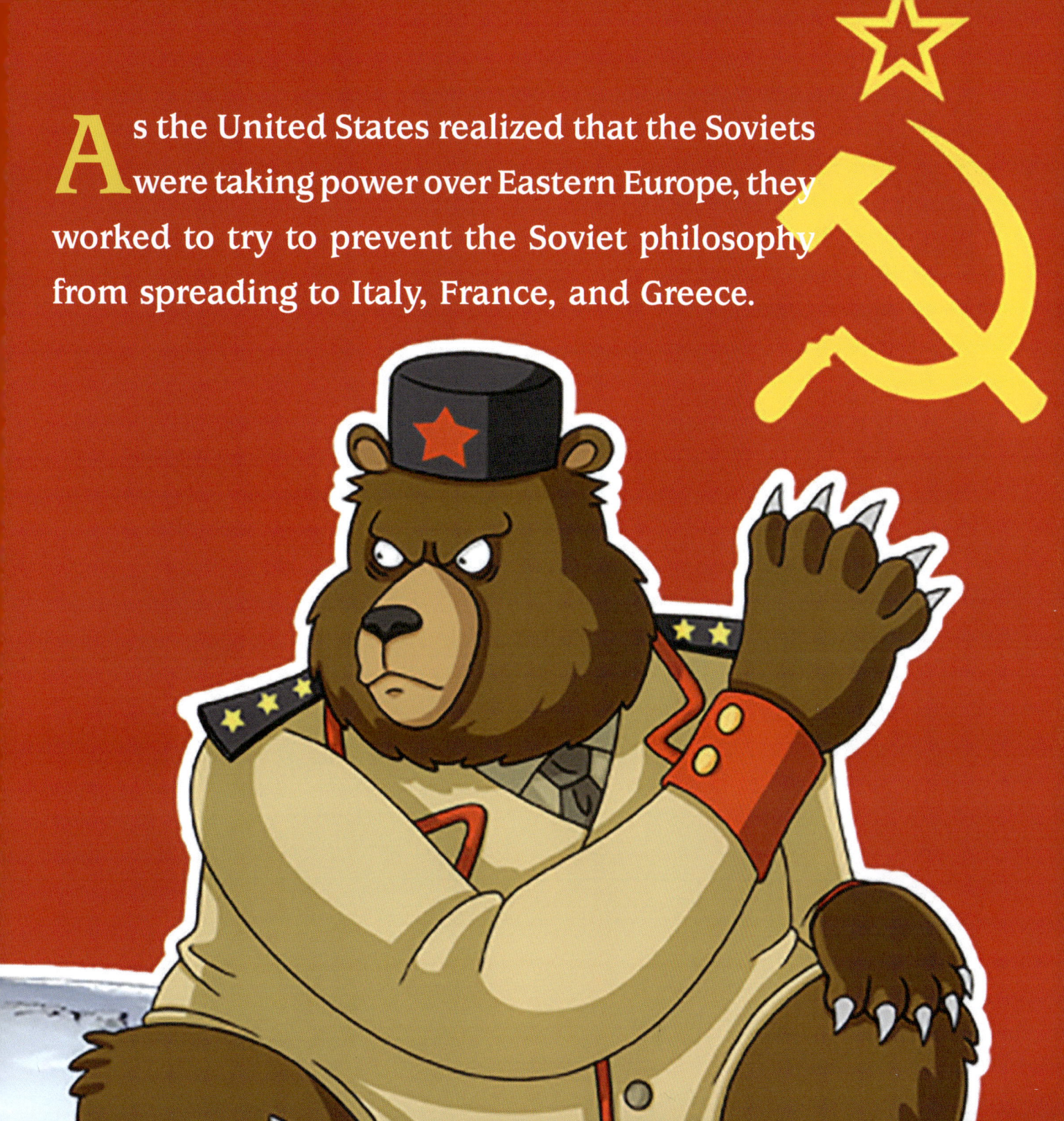

PREVENTING THE SPREAD OF COMMUNISM

The United States didn't want to get involved in European problems, however, the spread of communism was taken seriously. As early as 1947, the United States under the Truman Doctrine stated that it was the responsibility of the United States to curb the spread of communism. The U.S. pledged to give assistance to countries where communism was becoming a threat. The Marshall Plan, also in 1947, gave economic assistance in the billions to help governments become more stable so their democracies wouldn't be overthrown by the communists.

COMMUNIST FLAG

THE BLOCKADE OF BERLIN

When Berlin was divided up during the Potsdam Conference, sections of the city were being managed by the United States, England, and France. These sections were inside the communist-controlled lands of East Germany. In order to retaliate against the United States, the Soviets blocked all road traffic and railway access to the city.

This blockade began in 1948. The Cold War had now begun in earnest. Not to be outdone, the United States and Great Britain organized a huge

airlift to ensure that their areas received food and supplies. This airlift continued for 231 days until the Soviets lifted the blockade.

In 1949, the North Atlantic Treaty Organization, known as NATO, was formed when the United States joined with other countries to form a military and security alliance. NATO's mission was to halt the spread of communism. The Soviet Union reacted by joining with the now-communist governments in the eastern sections of Europe to form an opposing group by signing the Warsaw Pact in 1955.

TRUMAN SIGNING NORTH ATLANTIC TREATY

COLD WAR ALLIANCES

THE COLD WAR GOES WORLDWIDE

The dividing line between democratic and communist countries in Europe didn't change over the next few decades. However, other conflicts were breaking out all over the world in the continent of Asia, the continent of Africa, and the continent of South America. As long-established colonial governments began to fall, the superpowers became involved in proxy wars, each competing to take over the newly formed governments.

CHINESE COMMUNISTS

There had been a civil war raging between the nationalist Chinese and the communist Chinese since 1927. It re-ignited after World War II with the United States backing the nationalists and the Soviets backing the communists.

In 1949, the communists won this war. This brought further danger to democracies since China, the most populated country in the world, now had a communist government and was a Soviet ally.

THE FLAG OF NORTH KOREA

In 1950, the country of North Korea, which was communist controlled, attempted to overthrow South Korea. The United Nations and the United States sent military aid as well as troops. Both China and the Soviet Union gave their support to North Korea and the bloodshed of this proxy war continued for three years until a truce was agreed upon in 1953.

The following year, the French colonial government fell in the country of Vietnam and the stage was set for another proxy war to begin. The United States backed the government that was forming in South Vietnam and actually thwarted elections that might have led to a communist government taking a foothold in the region.

VIETNAM

NATIONAL LEADERS OF THE ANTI-COMMUNIST ALLIANCE, SEATO (SOUTHEAST ASIA TREATY ORGANIZATIONS) AT MANILA, PHILIPPINES.

To defend the area against the communist threat, the Southeast Asia Treaty Organization, called SEATO, was created in 1955. President Eisenhower dispatched over 700 military officers as well as economic assistance to the South Vietnamese government. However, by the time John F. Kennedy became president, the spread of communism there had not been stopped.

THE THREAT GETS CLOSER TO HOME

In 1959, Fidel Castro led a movement to overthrow the government in Cuba and replace it with a communist government. Castro soon turned to the Soviet Union for support. The Cold War of the United States and the Soviet Union was now very close geographically since the Soviets had a foothold that was only 90 miles from the coast of the state of Florida. The United States was under a more serious threat than before since the Soviets had intercontinental ballistic missiles.

FIDEL CASTRO (IN GREEN)

THE ARMS RACE

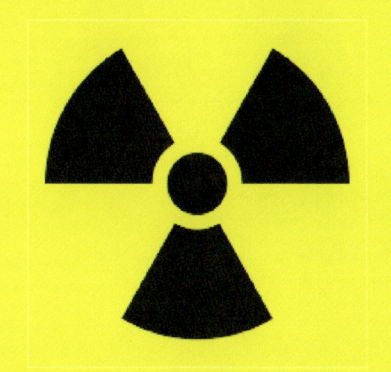

The United States had been the first country to create nuclear weapons during the Second World War. The U.S. dropped two atomic bombs on Japan at the end of the war in 1945 to ensure that Japan would surrender.

After the devastation in Japan, people all over the world could easily envision that a nuclear war between superpowers could potentially mean the end of civilization on Earth. To date, that was the only time that nuclear weapons have been used. However, during the Cold War, the United States and the Soviet Union began to stockpile vast quantities of nuclear weapons in an effort to show each other that they were strong enough to destroy each other if a war was started.

ATOMIC BOMBINGS OF
HIROSHIMA AND NAGASAKI

ATOMIC BOMB TEST

In 1949, the Soviet Union did its first test of an atomic bomb. The democratic countries around the world were frightened that the communists had nuclear capabilities. In 1952, the first hydrogen bomb was tested in the United States. This was a more powerful type of nuclear bomb than had been tested before. The Soviets continued to escalate the race by testing a powerful hydrogen bomb the next year.

During the 1950s, the United States and the Soviet Union both began to develop ICBMs, which is an acronym for Intercontinental Ballistic Missiles.

Peacekeeper Missile

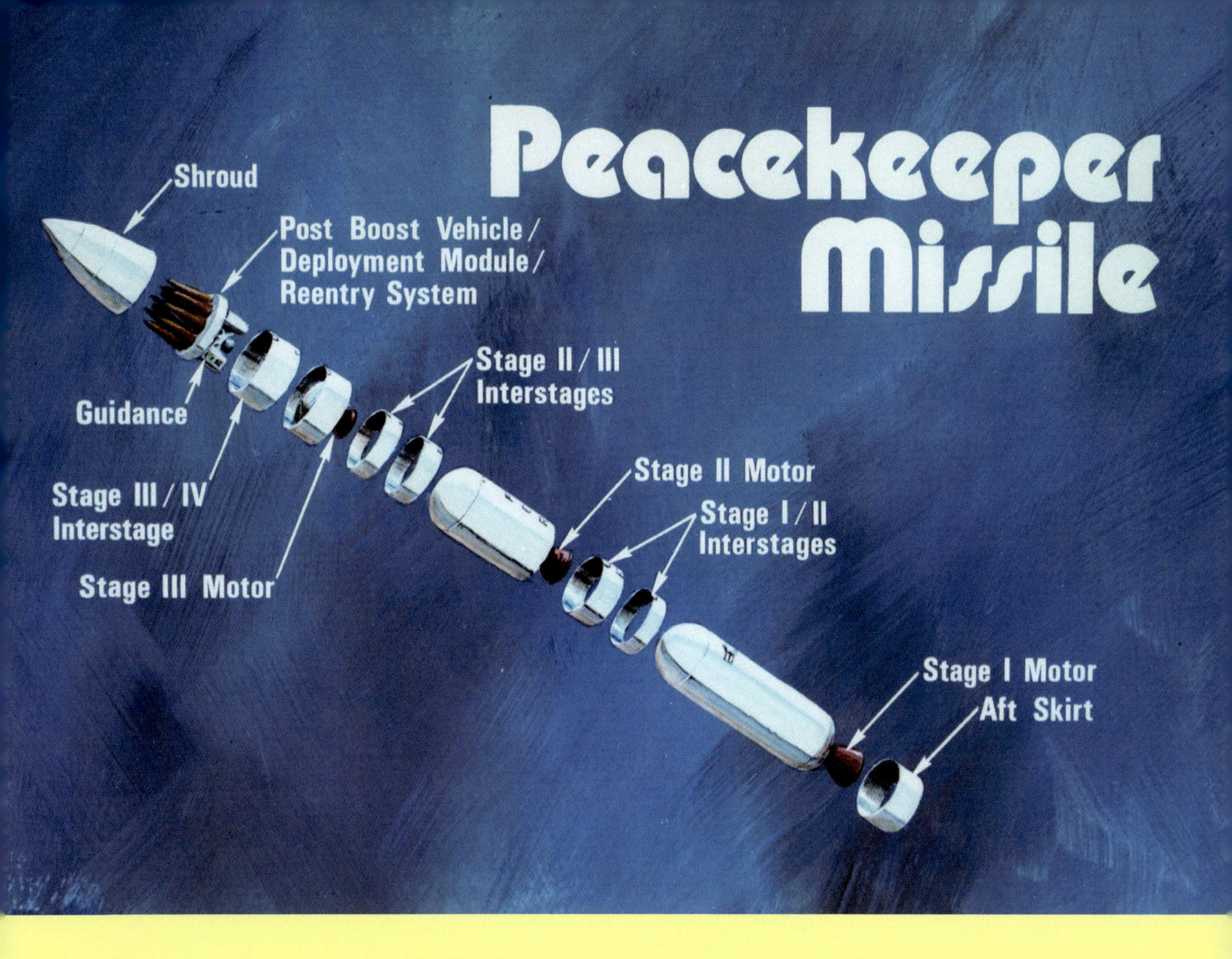

- Shroud
- Post Boost Vehicle / Deployment Module / Reentry System
- Guidance
- Stage II/III Interstages
- Stage III/IV Interstage
- Stage III Motor
- Stage II Motor
- Stage I/II Interstages
- Stage I Motor
- Aft Skirt

These missiles could be launched and hit a target 3,500 miles away with a nuclear warhead.

MISSILE LAUNCH ON WAKE ISLAND

DEFENSE MISSILES

As the Arms Race got more and more heated and both countries were spending billions to create their stockpile of weapons, people began to build underground bunkers so they might survive if there was a nuclear attack. The militaries in each government were working on defense missiles that could launch a counterattack on ICBMs before they were able to reach their targets. They built special arrays that were designed to detect incoming missiles.

MUTUAL ASSURED DESTRUCTION

When the stockpile of weapons and capabilities became equally matched on both sides there was talk of Mutual Assured Destruction, or MAD for short. If the Soviets launched an attack and the United States was destroyed, missiles from the United States would destroy the Soviet Union in retaliation. The same thing would happen if the U.S. sent an attack first.

MISSILE TEST

The cost of the mass destruction on both sides was too high because both countries would be destroyed. It kept the nuclear weapons in balance so neither side would take the first action to use them. This military doctrine of Mutual Assured Destruction was first developed during John F. Kennedy's administration.

LEONID BREZHNEV AND RICHARD NIXON TALKS IN 1973

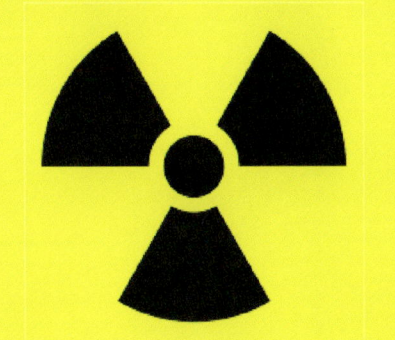

ARMS REDUCTION TALKS

By 1967, the United States had over 32,000 nuclear warheads and at one point the Soviet Union had 45,000. In the 1970s as the Arms Race continued, the rising costs of stockpiling weapons was having an effect on both countries. Talks began to ease the tensions. This event was called détente.

In May of 1972, President Richard Nixon signed the first of the SALT agreements with Soviet Leader Leonid Brezhnev. SALT stands for Strategic Arms Limitation Treaty. The goal of the treaty was to begin the reduction in the stockpile each side had of nuclear weapons.

When Ronald Reagan came into office in 1981, he initially opposed the SALT talks. However, his attitude shifted and by 1985, he was discussing the complete elimination of all such weapons. By 1988, there was a huge reduction in atomic weapons on both sides.

BREZHNEV AND NIXON SIGNING
THE SALT AGREEMENT

GEORGE BUSH AND MIKHAIL GORBACHEV

In July of 1991, President George H.W. Bush and Soviet leader Gorbachev approved the Strategic Arms Reduction Treaty or START that agreed upon the reductions of each stockpile of weapons. The Soviet Union collapsed in 1991 and it signaled the end of the Cold War and this dangerous time in world history.

The individual countries that were once part of the Soviet Union are continuing the arms reductions begun with START.

SUMMARY

The Cold War was begun at the end of the Second World War. The United States and the Soviet Union, who both fought together to overthrow Nazi Germany, became enemy superpowers. Democratic countries around the world didn't want communism to spread and were concerned as the Soviets grabbed up the countries of Eastern Europe and eventually aligned themselves with communist Cuba.

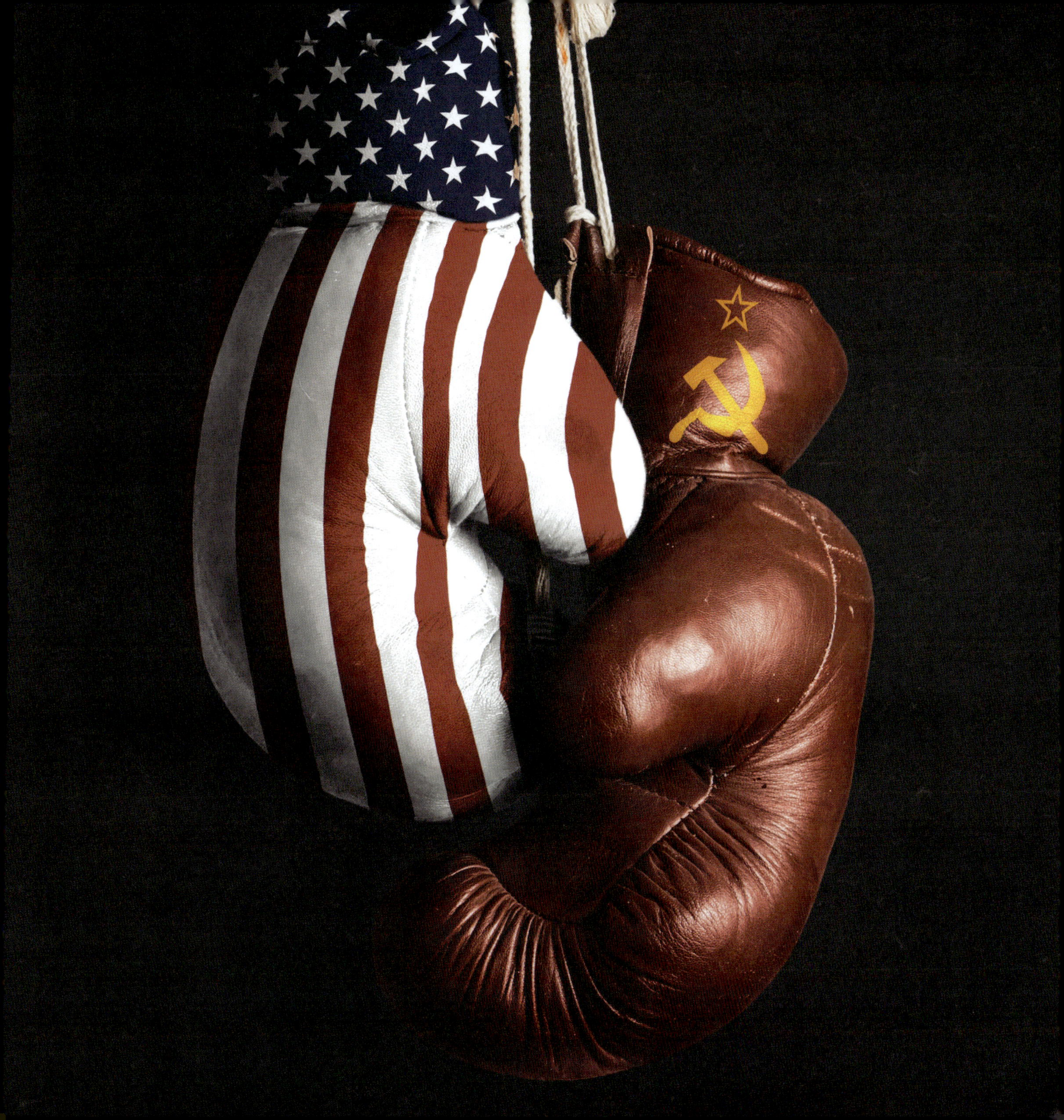

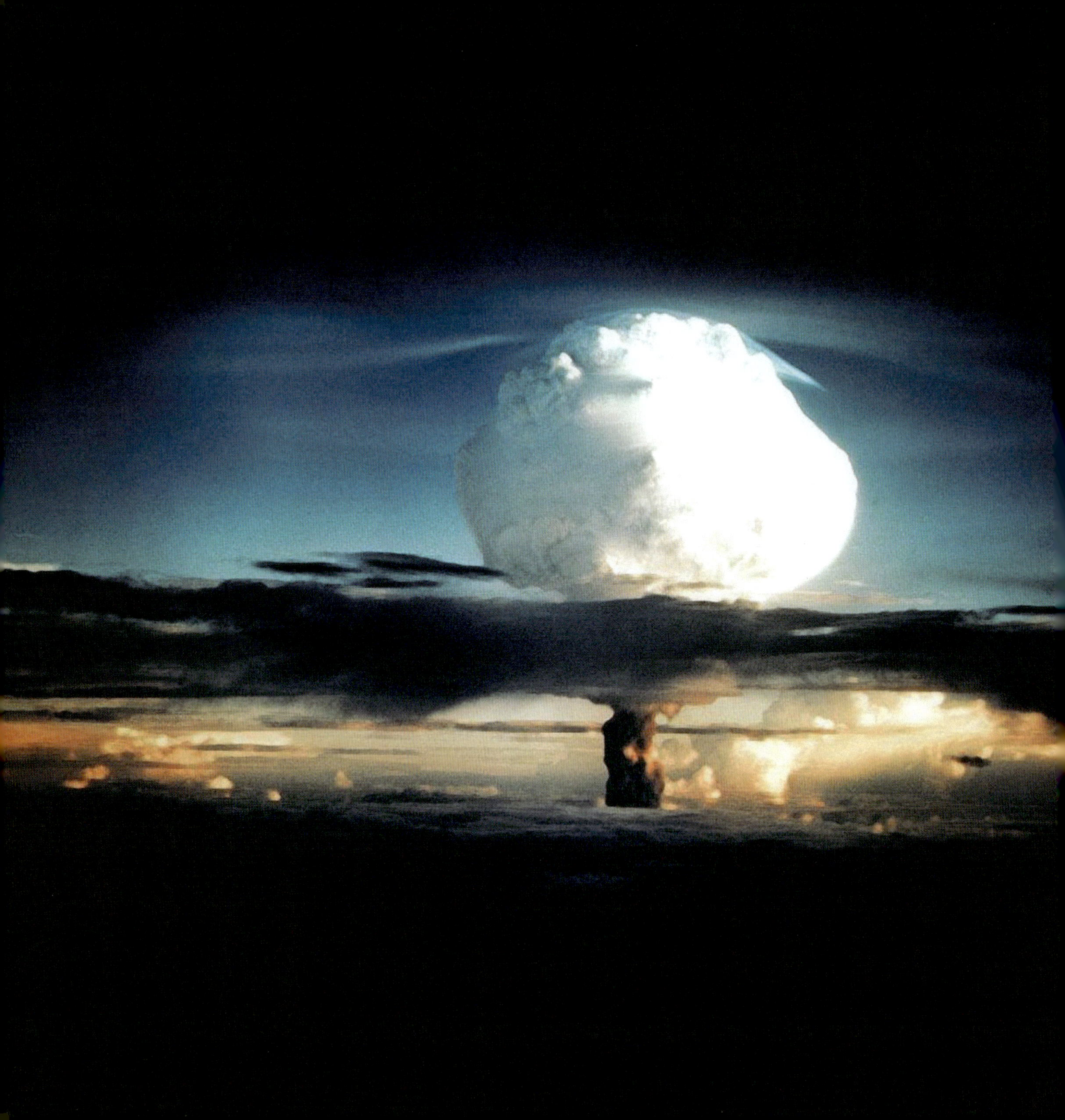

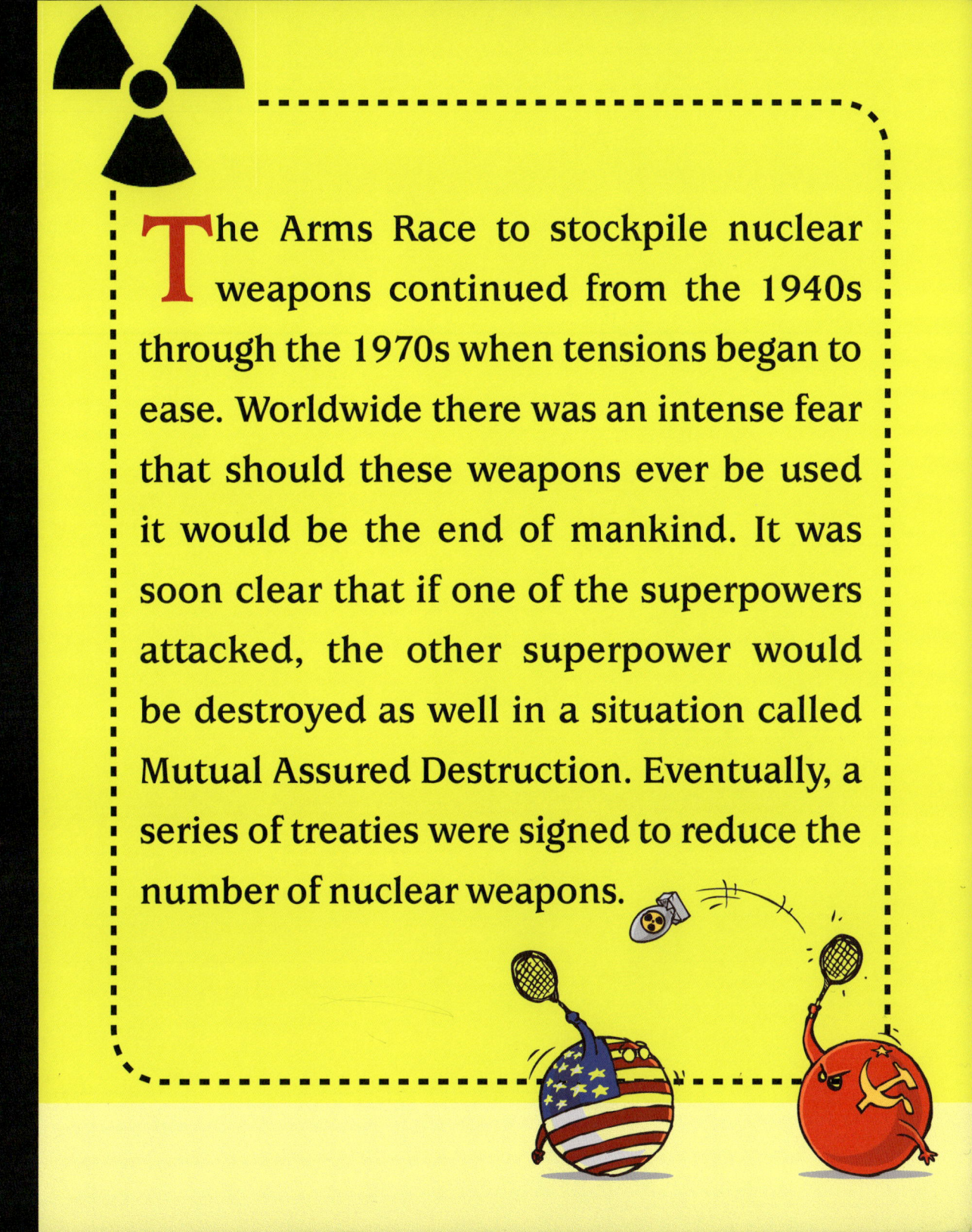

The Arms Race to stockpile nuclear weapons continued from the 1940s through the 1970s when tensions began to ease. Worldwide there was an intense fear that should these weapons ever be used it would be the end of mankind. It was soon clear that if one of the superpowers attacked, the other superpower would be destroyed as well in a situation called Mutual Assured Destruction. Eventually, a series of treaties were signed to reduce the number of nuclear weapons.

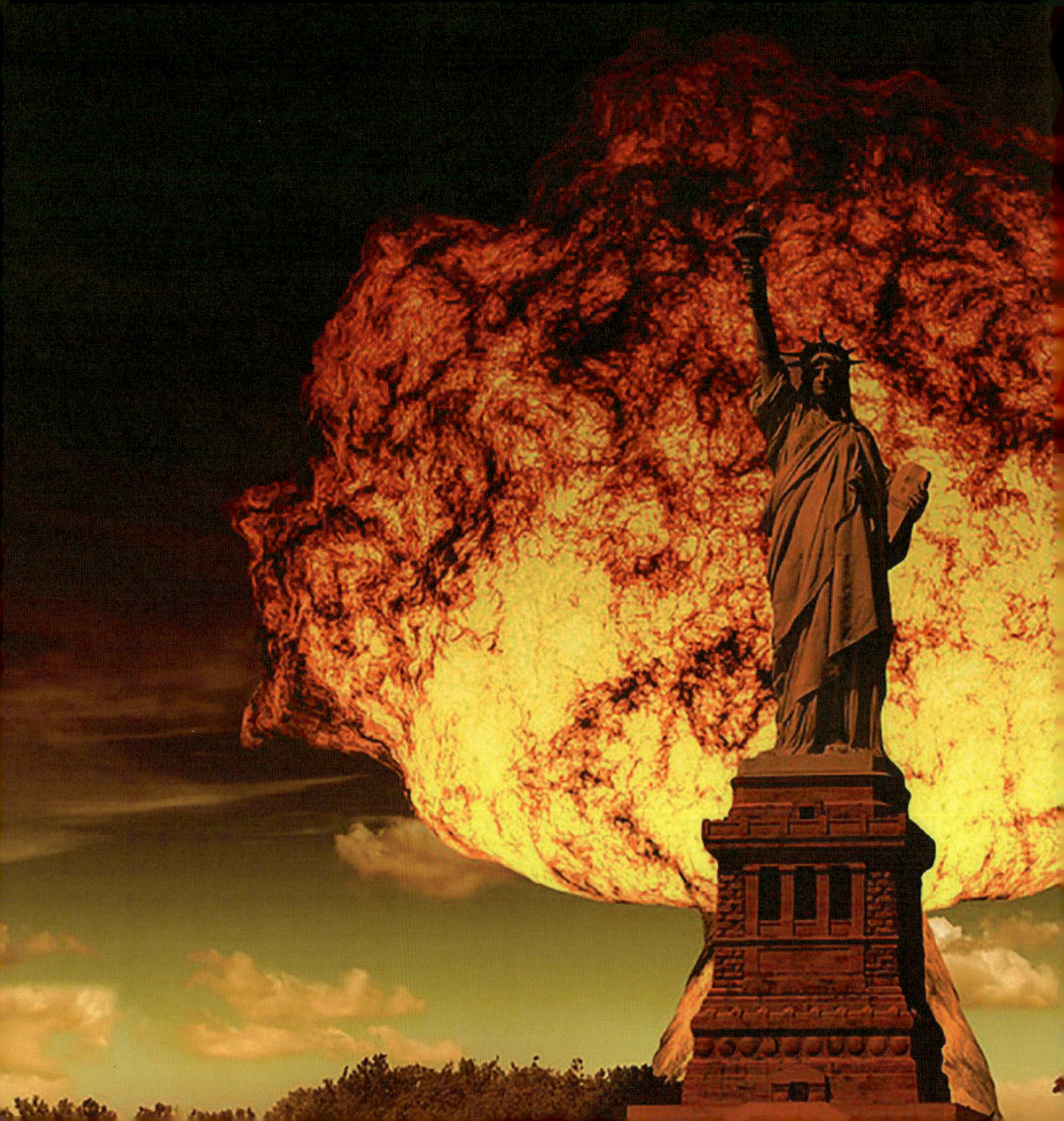

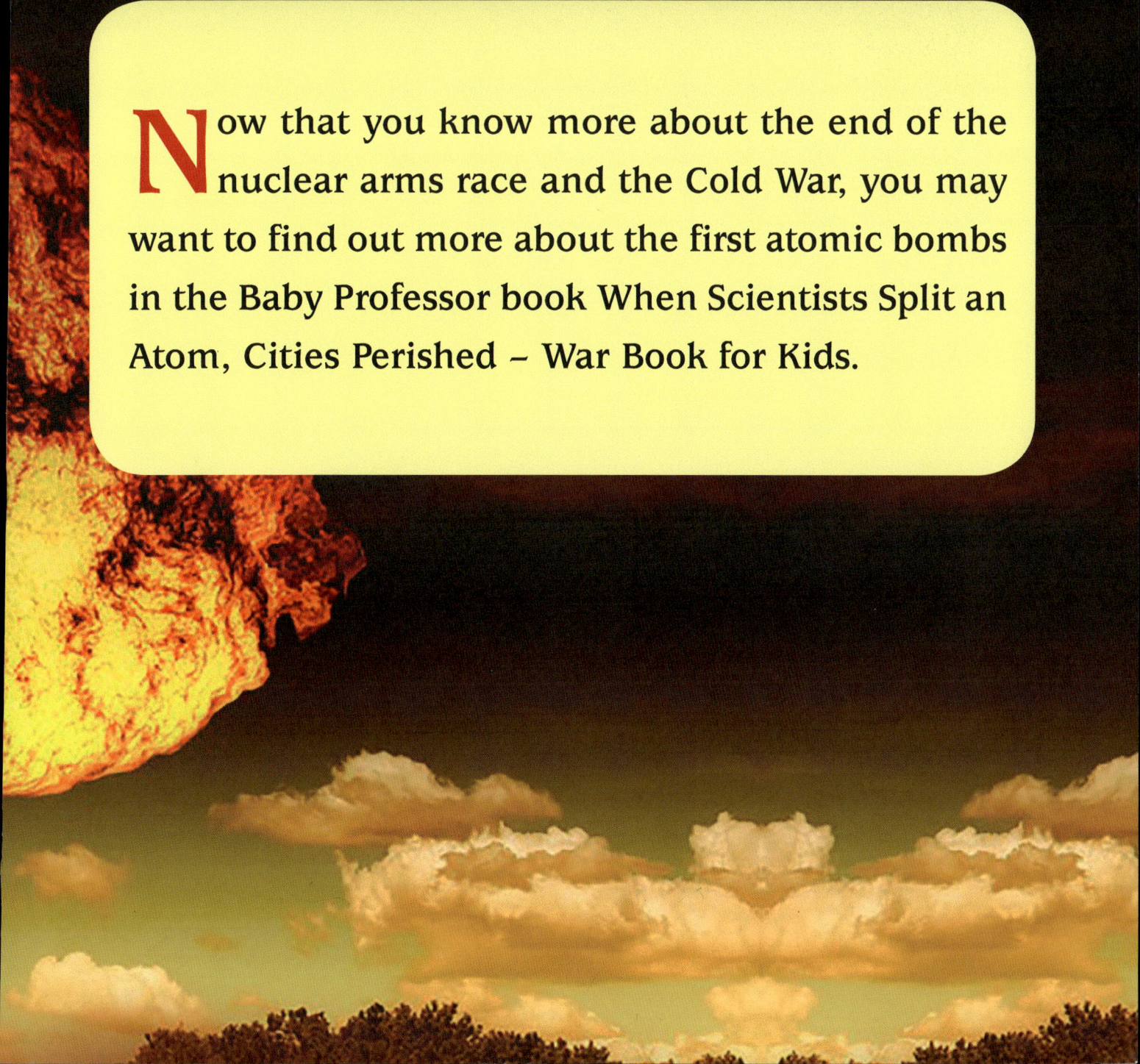

Now that you know more about the end of the nuclear arms race and the Cold War, you may want to find out more about the first atomic bombs in the Baby Professor book When Scientists Split an Atom, Cities Perished – War Book for Kids.

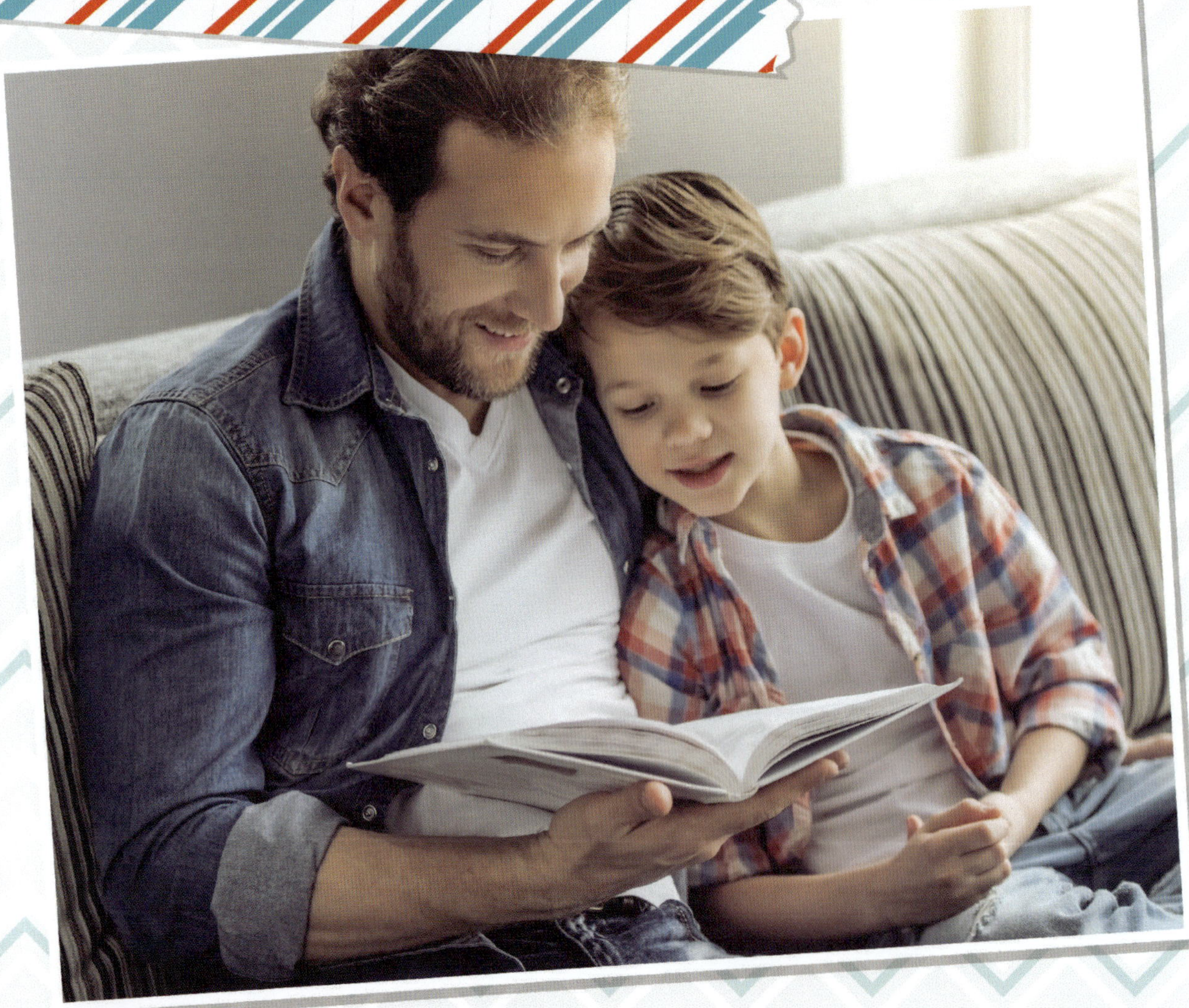

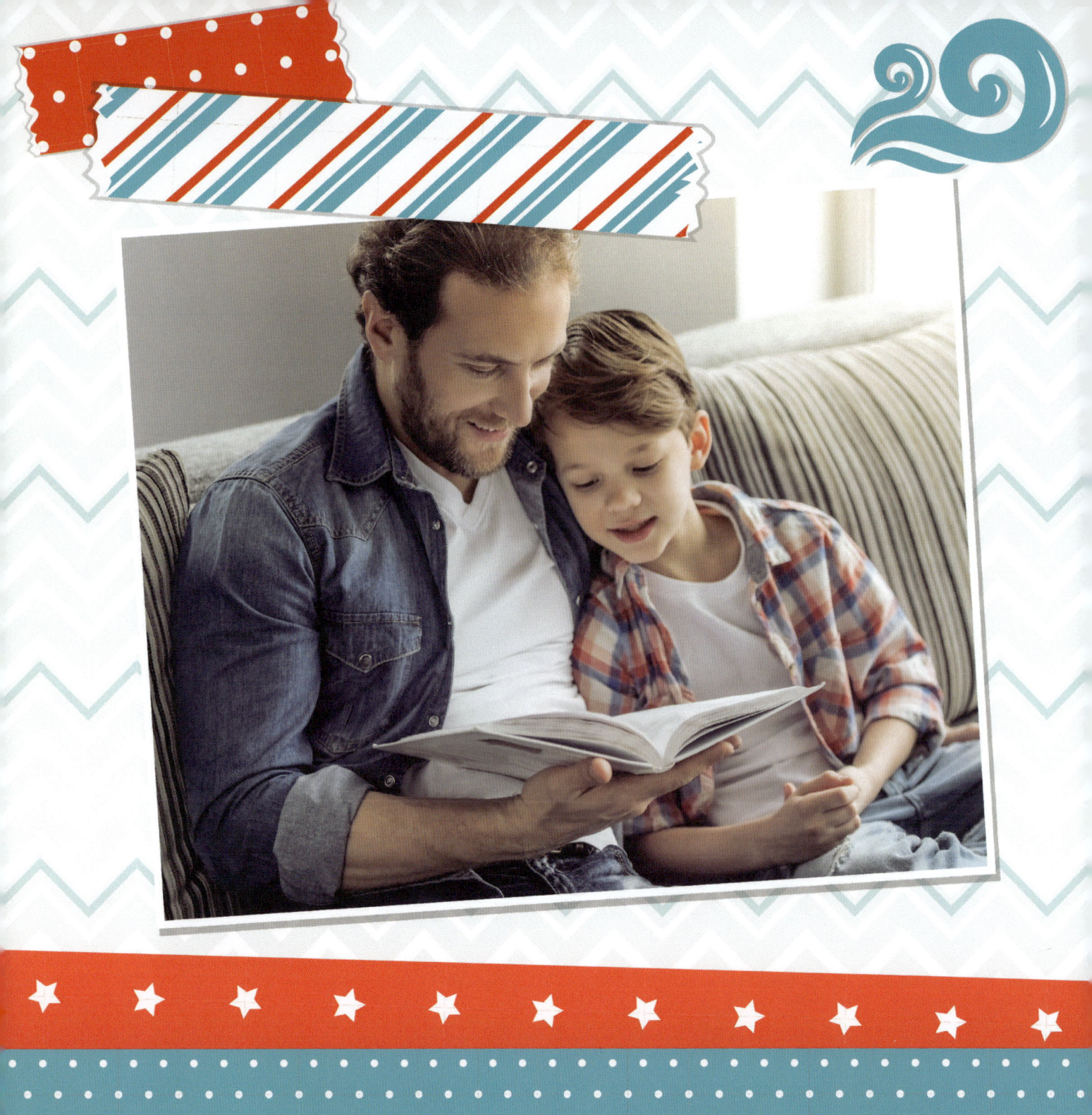

Visit

BABY PROFESSOR
EDUCATION KIDS

www.BabyProfessorBooks.com

to download Free Baby Professor eBooks
and view our catalog of new and exciting
Children's Books

Printed in Great Britain
by Amazon